If Some God Shakes Your House

Also by Jennifer Franklin

No Small Gift
Looming

If Some God Shakes Your House

Jennifer Franklin

Four Way Books
Tribeca

For Richard McCormick—
What will survive of us is love.

"death cannot harm me
more than you have harmed me,
my beloved life."

—Louise Glück

Library of Congress Cataloging-in-Publication Data

Names: Franklin, Jennifer, author.
Title: If some god shakes your house / Jennifer Franklin.
Description: New York : Four Way Books, [2023]
Identifiers: LCCN 2022033102 (print) | LCCN 2022033103 (ebook) |
ISBN 9781954245488 (paperback) | ISBN 9781954245495 (epub)
Subjects: LCGFT: Poetry.
Classification: LCC PS3606.R42234 I36 2023 (print) | LCC PS3606.R42234
(ebook) | DDC 811/.6--dc23/eng/20220715
LC record available at https://lccn.loc.gov/2022033102
LC ebook record available at https://lccn.loc.gov/2022033103

This book is manufactured in the United States of America and printed on
acid-free paper.

Four Way Books is a not-for-profit literary press. We are grateful for the assistance
we receive from individual donors, public arts agencies, and private foundations.

This publication is made possible with public funds from the
New York State Council on the Arts, a state agency.

NEW YORK STATE OF OPPORTUNITY. | **Council on the Arts**

PROUD MEMBER

[clmp]

We are a proud member of the Community of Literary Magazines and Presses.

Contents

As Antigone—

I'm not greedy. I will go
when I'm led from the city

to the tomb. I don't want
glory. They have never

understood me. It's not
a death wish that made me

tend to you, my love,
even though I knew

nothing could save you.
I couldn't let go—

our legs side by side,
as we slept, the flowers

you lined up in the soil,
after I picked them.

How you wouldn't accept
they were dead.

That planting them again
would not let them bloom.

As Antigone–

I buried the body at night
but knew I would still be caught.
The sky watched, a harder

shade of blue, as I knelt
above your lifeless body.
After I held dirt in my curved

palms, I couldn't return home
to the yellow sheets or eyelet
canopy. It didn't happen how

they described it—doing the deed
that doomed me to death.
It wasn't fast—over before

I could stop myself. It was deliberate.
I heard music—a deep lament
led me. I felt water but my mouth

remained dry. It held the words
anger and *apple.* You thought
I was going to say *soil* and *love.*

The wall of the city is high. Climbing,
I scrape my knees. When I see blood,
I believe I'm still alive. I know I will die.

Memento Mori: Greek Gold

Nothing organic remains. Wooden graves cradle
pomegranate beads, earrings, combs. You are familiar
with this ritual of adorning flesh with ornaments
that will outlast us. Gold diadems and crowns host two cicadas
and a bee. Untouched in plastic cases, they perch on grey velvet
stands. The gods the Greeks cherished now cherish us, our greedy
stares and Protean desires. The earth chooses to preserve what it
cannot use. Open tombs reveal strewn jewels and dried fruit.

You poke at cold pieces, imposing desire onto corpses
you cannot see. You love what you want them to have been.
This is one version of an afterlife. You can't dwell on the dead
any longer and leave to buy replicas of bronze baubles that hung
from each branch of their bodies. You smell the faint aroma
of what they once parted their lips to taste.

Memento Mori: Bird Head

A suitable end to February—waking and drawing
the blinds to discover a bird's head, stuck by its own blood
to the sill, outside the window. Thirty-three floors up, a hawk
devoured the body on the roof and discarded the eyeless head.
Its beak, long and curved, looks like the Venetian plague
doctor's mask that hung on a red velvet ribbon in my first
apartment. The head sits, stubborn, a reminder of what
this winter has taken and what remains three weeks before spring.

As soon as I roll a newspaper and push the head off the ledge
to the stubby shrubs below, I regret it. The dried blood,
still smeared on the gray stone, resembles a daub of paint
a child tried to scrape from her thumb. On my first
organ donor form, I checked off each box except *eyes*,
as if there were some way to see, even after death.

February

Our long coats are all that separate us from the cold. Halfway around the world, the sky opens to put out wildfires over the carcasses of burned marsupials. We wait for the subway, for the train. My daughter waits for her short yellow bus that arrives each morning with one sobbing boy. Politicians preen and posture; the air is damp with acquittal. We bend our heads but not in prayer. Our palms hold small backlit tablets that promise information and escape. Miles north, a student paints a swastika in my old dorm. Another student covers it with a star. Only the dog is calm, sleeping in a circle in her clean fleece bed. Orwell wrote, "There was truth and there was untruth, and if you clung to the truth even against the whole world, you were not mad." I try to put my daughter to sleep on time in her new room. As I read the familiar incantations, flowers climb up the lamp to the ceiling. All the animals have escaped the zoo. I want the story to end there. All of them tucked into the corners of the zookeeper's room—breathing their heavy eucalyptus breath across the night. Their fur shining in the moonlight through the blinds.

As Antigone—

I consider my father. He was always
restless—waiting for the fate he knew

would find him. He never understood
why he was still unsatisfied even after

he bought the suburban house and the car
he coveted. As he sat at the head

of the table next to his wife, who dyed
her hair as soon as she started to gray,

he couldn't recognize her. Only the dog
didn't cower at his moods, changeable

as the sea. As he broke the rack
on the pool table in the basement

or carved the roast as we sat down
for dinner, we felt his silent resentment.

Even before he turned his knife
to his own eyes, I saw how he struggled

to keep it still. As the sun set in the cold
kitchen, we told him stories of our day—

showed him the smartest version of ourselves.
We believed that, along with mother's dark

beauty, we could make him happy. He didn't
see us. His eyes focused on the planter

outside the glass door with the dying
hibiscus—wilted, closed to the sunset.

Even as girl, alone mixing broken acorns
with sticks in the woods behind school,
you believed you were more important
than you were. Birds know they are only part
of a flock, flecking the sky with feathers.

Memento Mori: Moth

You stand in the early morning light of the hallway
thirty-three floors above the traffic inching below us.
When you grab the moth, I don't know what to do.
My mouth falls as open as the elevator door
we're about to enter. You hold it as it struggles.
I startle you when I call your name and you release it.
It must be injured; its thin, taupe wings are between
your fingers again. *Let go of the butterfly.*

(You never accepted the word moth and have no use
for synonyms.) I can't tell if you understand me
or if you let go on your own. Everything's like this
with us; I know next to nothing. I cannot forget
your face as you pinch the fluttering wings,
oblivious to the suffering you cause.

Memento Mori: Wind Phone

You don't yet know
that I take care
of every weak thing.
You wait to tell me
your bad news until
you're leaving as if
you can bear only
so much consolation.

If you speak your grief
as the gray-haired farmers
and fisherman do
on the phone connected
to nothing, you may
never stop calling the wind.

Memento Mori: Red First, Always

What you want to see in my hand. Finally, I open.
Each small aperture a wound, each flourish a Corinthian
column of desire. Your room, every shade of gray—
oyster shells, unlocked. Once, we saw a red tulip, stuck
in mid-bloom, trapped in acrylic. You knew it was more real
to me than the petals I pass without bending to them.
You teach me to look after years of not. Your stare
so unbearable, I force myself not to turn away or close my eyes.

Like holding a blossom that becomes the whole world,
there is nothing outside this quiet room. When you
touch me, thousands of flowers fall from your fingertips.
Your fan hangs motionless from the ceiling, suspended
like our bodies in time, suspended like the question neither
of us wants to answer. Love, one of us is always leaving.

May

It happens slowly, while we are in the kitchen preparing cannellini beans and kale. The smoke alarm is about to go off. The dog is pacing; my daughter is crying. She cannot tell us what hurts. She has no words to describe her suffering. Maybe none of us do. I was born twenty-eight days before Roe v. Wade. On paper, I always had the right to choose. Pregnant at twenty-six, in the hospital with hyperemesis (the same condition that killed Charlotte Brontë) an IV drip protruded from my right arm. As doctors tried to stop my vomiting and weight loss, my mother and my husband talked me out of the abortion. Fear was their shared weapon—he threatened me, she predicted he would stop loving me. I had the baby; he stopped loving me anyway.

The news is an active volcano. We listen but we go about our lives. We sign petitions, make phone calls, march, send online donations. Yet we eat the kale and beans, curl or straighten our hair, bring the dog for long walks in the park. We know where this is headed. We hold each other's hands, make promises. We still believe we are good but I cannot sleep without pills.

The new season of *The Handmaid's Tale* is about to start, so reporters ask Margaret Atwood about abortion legislation. "Once you take your first breath, it's out the window with you."

As a child, I read on the swing set with my dog as my mother made dinner. She never liked cooking but I didn't know that then. The sun set over the bike path and I thought if I could find a way out of the suburbs to the city, I would be happy. The dog's head on my lap and my book were my comfort. I live in the city now. I have my books and another dog's head in my lap. My daughter is crying. The doctors cannot help her. Her father is a surgeon; he refuses to pay for her once she turns twenty-one though she will never be able to wash herself or live alone. Her father hasn't seen her in six years. She will be a life-long toddler. I love her, so he still controls me.

As Antigone—

I consider my mother. Until she died,
I couldn't admit she had flaws.

She always put on a brave face,
a good show. Even in the morning,

she was cheerful—singing
to wake us for school, making us

laugh as she served cinnamon toast.
I worshiped her as she stood

in her silk robe by the window.
Perhaps the prophecies made her

anxious and controlling. Maybe
she realized who her husband was

only after it was too late. She turned
all her attention to me. With so much

scrutiny, nothing could thrive.
Everything she liked, I had to like.

She dragged me to antique shows,
bought me old dolls in blue boxes—

babies swaddled in pink, stuck
with a vague scent of powder. Three

sizes of *Little Women* with long dresses
and hard, musty hair. Their eyes stared

from white wicker shelves all night
as I slept. She didn't start loving me

until my life unraveled, helpless
as I was at birth when I disappointed

her with my one blonde eyelash.
Her experiment failed. It was impossible

to tell if that saddened or comforted
her. Her face remained inscrutable

as the rows of marble busts that line
the walls of my favorite museum.

You are as stubborn as your father and will not listen. You want bulbs to transform in their soil to emerge as different flowers.

As Antigone—

I am tired of everyone
telling me what to do.

For as long as I can remember
my mother told me how

I should feel, what to eat,
who to date, what clothes

looked good (and bad)
on my shape—which colors

I could pile in front of stunned
cashiers. During the first

hurricane, she said I would die
if I didn't listen to her orders.

I grew up confusing opinion
with oracle. She reminded me

all men are dangerous, each time
I left the house alone. Even after

I moved four states away for college,
she sent me newspaper clippings—

warnings in the mail. She believed
I was safely married to a surgery

resident and drove five hours
to sit by my hospital bed and watch

as IV fluids hydrated me.
That winter, I wanted to end

my pregnancy, after losing
thirty-three pounds in seven weeks.

She joined my husband's campaign
to keep me sick and expecting.

I visit a friend I haven't seen in years,
and confide how afraid I am

for my disabled daughter when I'm dead.
Her husband tells me my daughter

is happy and oblivious and *she*
wouldn't know if she were being raped

as if she has less sentience than a dog
chained to a pole in an overgrown yard.

Memento Mori: Central Park Polar Bear

After reading that he died, I am relieved. For twenty-seven years,
he swam laps all day, slicing the water. His seven hundred pounds—
muscle, tendon, yellowing fur, black eyes—all turned to ash.
The week you were diagnosed, I pushed your stroller thirty-three blocks
to the zoo. You recognized him from your board book and flapped
your arms to imitate his strokes. Unseasonably warm for October,
I stood, stunned inside my black sweater—embroidered
with flowers of forgetfulness. Watching in front of his small tank,

was I the only one who saw how sad it was that he barreled in backstrokes
of figure eights? His giant paws slashed the cloudy water, knowing
he would never get anywhere despite how hard he tried. Eleven years later,
you still run back and forth in our living room, with or without music,
babbling your indecipherable language. Your swimmers shoulders cut
the empty air all night as you make patterns on the threadbare rug.

Memento Mori: Doll, 1983

I wasn't the one who found what the neighborhood boys did
to my Cindy Sue doll, as my brother watched, after they tried
to get me to follow them down the steep stairs to our basement.
I knew from their faces they weren't going down there to play
board games—stacked on the shelves my father built when he
wasn't in the office—or even the Nintendo, hooked up to the old TV.
I stayed upstairs finishing homework but heard the boys laughing.
My mother found the five-foot doll—naked and face down.

Jagged cuts of bright red marker slashed her where her underwear
should have been. I was too young to understand what they we trying
to do to this plastic version of girls they knew. When my mother told
my hot-faced brother those boys could not come back, fear found me
like the basement's musty smell that always stayed on our clothes
even after we walked upstairs and shut the door.

Memento Mori: Mother after My Treatment

When she returns to her garden, it fills her with sorrow.
She didn't know it would become wild so soon. She might
never coax it back from this ruined form. Only the animals
scavenging for bulbs seem familiar. How quickly the earth
forgets how fast one can leave the world. Rose of Sharon
blooms above the hosta—top-heavy, improbable. Weeds overtake
each bed, and the Japanese lanterns that her neighbor's dead mother
planted, creep under the fence and spread like disease.

In the city, as she changed my trach dressing, something
washed away with my wound. She is unfamiliar to herself, weeding
potted plants on her patio. She's not at home in her old house
or in my small apartment where we shared a bed. Only daylilies
bloom the way she remembers them. Their orange faces promise
it's not too late to salvage something before the summer is gone.

June

I watched the news and walked out of my childhood home for the last time. I didn't look back at the pink and orange hibiscus—their huge stamen reaching for the sky. I didn't see the brown door, sun-stained and blotched, desperate for a new coat of paint. I studied the grass, unnaturally green, admonishing the footpath. House of excuses, house of apologia.

When Goya, deaf, retreated to the *Quinta del Sordo* outside Madrid, it already had its name. The man who lived there before was also deaf. I studied Lucia Joyce's schizophrenia in Dublin, eight years before my daughter was born and didn't know my child's mind would bear a similar affliction. The girl who lived in our apartment before us had pervasive developmental disorder and an aquarium with tropical fish. She watched their colors as they swam back and forth all day. The young man who's moving in has Asperger's and will be cared for by his twin sister down the hall. My daughter spends her life watching puppets' bright fur as they sing and dance across three screens. Perhaps Nietzsche was right when he theorized eternal return.

By most accounts, Goya, at 74, painted the black paintings for himself. Some scholars claim they are frauds painted by his son, Javier. All that matters is their testimony to our brutality while we inhabit lives we never thought possible. Milgram proved how easy it is to obey, to push the buzzer. Judith beheading Holofernes does not frighten me;

I watched Saturn devour my child for nine years and now I watch as children suffer behind bars. When I close my eyes, all I see is Goya's drowning dog. He's stuck like Winnie in *Happy Days* but without speech. All that gold light above the quicksand—as if nothing can save us.

July

The night we plan our move from 103rd Street to 102nd Street, we eat at a picnic table in Riverside Park with our daughter and our dog. I lived on these same two streets with my first husband and my dog twenty-three years earlier. I recall Martha Nussbaum's lectures on eternal return and watch the fireflies flit. Our daughter sees them and murmurs "eyes." She takes your hand and brings it to her lips, something she never did to her father whose foul moods and stern commands frightened her.

Louise Bourgeois writes about her first sculptures—"At the dinner table when I was very little, I would hear people bickering. To escape the bickering, I started modelling the soft bread with my fingers. With the dough of the French bread—sometimes it was still warm—I would make little figures."

Walking up the hill from the picnic tables, the unseasonal breeze feels like the end of summer on my childhood bike path, just days before school. You catch a firefly to show our daughter but she has moved on. She wears her Joan of Arc expression that she donned at the fireworks two days earlier. As if the world were an illusion that none but she can fathom.

As Antigone—

I hesitate when I look
at the dog. I don't want her

to see me like this—
crying and incapable

of comforting her. Nobody
answers relentless calls

for help. When one
is most needy, one is most

alone. The ones I love
will go on with their little lives—

reading, running,
fucking. They won't just

get by; they'll be happy.
Even the dog will forget me.

Memento Mori: Death Mask

When I saw his face set in white
plaster, mounted on black velvet
in a chipped walnut frame, I knew
I had to have this cheap replica
from his final room in Rome.
To hang the stark mold above
my desk and study his ever-closed eyes
and the shape of his last living mouth.

When I first read his work, I didn't know
he died doubting it, or that his friend denied him
hidden morphine that would have eased
his death. I did not yet know how dying feels—
how painful and posthumous to stare at a blue
ceiling—lungs full of water, enough to drown.

Memento Mori: Preparing to Move

They're finally leaving me—each old good thought—
my favorite park with the dead dog and all the calm days
in countries you promise to unruin for me. I hide my soap,
a brush, and fleece in your rooms and tell you I want to bring
nothing else but my books, my dead grandmother's marble table,
and her intarsia desk. But you don't believe me. You think I covet
cabinets stuffed with souvenirs—churches caught under snow
globes, giraffes scratched on banana paper, dancers smothered
in porcelain lace. You worry I want to pack boxes deep as caves.

You don't understand that when I lay in a machine for seven weeks,
as oncologists irradiated my sliced tongue and slashed neck,
I learned to walk out of my home and close the door
as if I were not coming back. You don't know each day blooms
into leave-taking. That when I say *goodbye*, I mean it.
That all words will always be practice for *no*.

August

The train tunnels towards me and I brace myself each time it opens. Every train is the one that struck Anna Karenina or the one that killed the boy who flung himself on the tracks where I teach. Every train I see reminds me of the ones that stopped at the concentration camps and led millions to death. I watch another documentary. Young German Neo-Nazis sit at the site of the Wannsee Conference and defend what their grandfathers did. The former historian forgets history and refuses to see everything that happened and is continuing to happen now at the border, in our own streets. In *Antigone*, Sophocles wrote, "Oh it's terrible when the one who does the judging judges things all wrong."

Antigone wanted to lie down thigh to thigh with her brother. She was the first to understand that there are lives worse than death. My child looks into my face and feels the only safety she will know. Her father hated me because I would not abandon her, but his betrayal gave me this gift of my new life. With him, I watched a bestiary of animals roam free in the Mara. Now, giraffes and elephants are dying off. Lions are being hunted for their teeth to make coveted necklaces. Twenty-three years ago, just the rhino was endangered as we explored Kenya, oblivious to suffering. We did not claw at each other in the Sahara—he learned nothing from nature except how to leave a zebra carcass, picked clean in the sand.

I join my daughter's school trip to the ballet. The dancer grips the stage with her bare feet. She twists her small body into that shape so many times, she convinces herself it doesn't hurt. That's what I did when I lived with him—erased my needs until I could no longer ignore the small voice of the hostage inside me. I don't sit by the window on the train. I cannot see where my daughter is headed. The Hudson runs sharp in morning light.

As Antigone—

If you think I wasn't angry
at his betrayal—you're wrong.
Fury moved through my body

with the gravity of a waterfall.
I cut my ankles under my dress
where no one would see.

I snuck out of my room at 3 a.m.
wearing ripped nightclothes
under my winter coat, not knowing

what I would tell my brother
of this ruin. Once I discovered
home was a lie I told myself,

I shoveled the dirt to bury my life.
The moon watched without judgment—
knowing nothing ever changes

except the clothes men wear while
they wound. Your light, through
the branches, shines like a paper lantern.

As Antigone—

Even without moonlight,
I still see the two brown horses
standing by the fence

across the road from my first
house. In late summer, grass
grows tall around the posts.

For weeks, I did not leave
except to unlatch the mailbox
and walk with the sheepdog

back to the empty yellow house.
Those rooms watched ghosts
fly from bodies of the living.

Those fields opened to take
bulbs from my hands. Once,
a turkey vulture emerged

and frightened the dog on the deck
as pine trees admonished the creek.
In the spring, flowers clustered

in small patches. Tulips top-heavy
with shame, tipped in the wind.
One owl watched from the broken elm.

The moon remembers the waif I was
and watched my wrist pull the red
damask curtains closed for the night.

Memento Mori: Annunciation, without Angel

Look at me—I was already acquainting myself
with anguish. I was not special. I sensed
doom that first instant—your heavy weight
in my arms, umbilical cord still joining us,
your grown body draped over me like a cloying
velvet curtain—eyes fastened skyward, always
looking through me. I should have said *no*,
should have run away, ended it all.

But I could not turn down all of that love.
Too late, I found it was not worth it. God
does not take no for an answer. If I had refused,
it would have ended the same. But then I could
wear some scar of comfort that mine were not
the hands that married you off to wood, to ruin.

Memento Mori: Volcano

Across Naples from Vesuvius,
Solfatara looms, tempting tourists to walk
its treacherous sides. A young boy ignores
the fence and ignites; his father burns to death
trying to save him. His mother follows,
drowns in quicksand. Their other son watches
from a distance. He will never forget
the moment his family married fire.

He will always remember their screams and how
the air smelled as he watched them disappear—
the ferocious mouths of fantasy book dragons,
finally real. The way fire is only itself.
It's as if he were always an orphan—and their death
fated for the bluest day of September.

September

After the hurricane came the hurricane. Three women willing to ruin their lives. First, there was a heat wave, then the cold came without warning. We buckled sandals on our feet one day, slipped them into boots the next. Coats hung lonely on the backs of chairs. We whispered the news to each other so the children wouldn't know how angry we were to hear *rape* called *horseplay*.

Hannah Arendt wrote, "In an ever-changing, incomprehensible world the masses had reached the point where they would, at the same time, believe everything and nothing, think that everything was possible and that nothing was true."

The man I loves rarely drinks. Yet he has taken to ordering gin. I ask him if he's thinking of Winston Smith. He says he's thinking of getting through the next two years. My daughter holds his hand on the way home from the restaurant. This court will rule her rights away. Still, we walk the rain-soaked sidewalks to the lit building by the river. The lights are on for the dog who waits in a circle in her grey bed. My girl skips down the wide avenue. For once, I am relieved she cannot read or understand the story on everyone's lips.

As Antigone—

I visit the psychiatric hospital, and the guard
confiscates the small spiral-bound notebook

I bought her at the dollar store. The pink
plastic cord could be pulled from the pages

and used to injure herself, he explains,
I should have known not to bring it.

Magazines with smiling women in swimsuits
are sanctioned, as if they will teach her

how to look happy. The music I transfer
to a small silver device makes it in

but does not please her. Vacant, she gazes
past me, her thick hair twisted in a bun.

She's more beautiful than she was
at her wedding. She begs me to get her out

of the locked ward. Says she cannot sleep
one more night in this place. The doctor asks

if I brought a word search but finding nouns
in a field of scattered letters cannot fix this.

How can I tell her I know the corners
of chaos where her mind has lured

and trapped her? How can I unpeel myself
from this vinyl loveseat and leave her

with leering nurses and patients? How
can I turn around and press the buzzer

for the guard to open the door and let me
walk out again into the strange July sun?

How many ways have you invented to harm yourself?
How many times did you wonder if you should be locked up?

As Antigone—

I didn't have a choice.
I wasn't trying to be good.

I could not brush my hair
each morning if you were lying

on the ground. *Three girls ago*,
I would have run from this—

buried myself in books and velvet
dresses. Laced my boots so tight,

I could not have recognized
my name. Anyone can throw

a corpse below ground. It takes love
to prepare a body for the earth.

It was not courage; I couldn't
listen to the violin while you lay

speechless. I could use the scarf
I wore to hide my scars

for seven weeks at the cancer center—
leave a clean corpse. The daisies,

fat faces stuck in full bloom,
would watch me close my eyes.

Memento Mori: Colony Collapse

I used to think Dickinson covered everything
about bees but now they're disappearing. More
alarming news competes for my attention
but my mother won't let me forget the bees.
Her garden is almost empty of them. I learn about
their plight—abandoned queens, pesticides, parasites,
pathogens. Even her *mystic illusion dahlia* cannot coax
more than two small bees around their buttery blooms.

Worried, she warns—*nothing will survive without them.*
I read the headlines—lists of man-made horrors
I cannot itemize. Funeral after funeral of those who,
struggling to breathe, called out for their mothers.
I think of the insects in Dutch still lifes. The bees lie
upturned on the table, their five eyes, all closed.

Memento Mori: Apple Orchard

In the gold light of early October, we climb
the orchard hills searching empty trees
for apples. The boy at the gate tells us Ida Red,
Rome, Crispin, and Surprise are all ripe
and ready for our hands. We walk and walk.
The dog investigates every fallen apple
with her frantic nose. Even as we savor
this autumn's sunlight of our beginning,
headlines remind us what is lost. Large families
have picked the trees clean, leaving plastic
bottles and paper napkins blowing like white flags.
Instead of the fragrant apples on the ground
reminding me of my mother's baking,
I catch the smell of decay.

I catch the smell of decay.
as we walk through so many rows
of stubby trees that we cannot find our way
back to the car. We do not say what we're thinking—
if we leave without a single apple, it might mean
what we have done to the earth cannot be undone.
The children who grow up on this imperiled planet
will not remember pulling the russet fruit
from the branches to bite into its sweet flesh. We see

boys throw bruised apples at each other. Still children,
they already know what is damaged becomes a weapon.
As we pull away, we watch them run the worn paths.
Their masks fall as they bend to collect
the blemished apples and fill their empty bags.

October

I try to keep the image of the sunset over the lighthouse at the edge of the Cape but the tornadoes we drove away from, on our way home, erase it from my mind. We never reached the lighthouse. The white-headed dog got sunstroke and collapsed in the sand. We hitched a ride back to the bed & breakfast. I hold the few people I love in my fist like the wooden tulips I bought myself one Mother's Day. News inserts itself into my sleep—the faces of judges who should not judge, children still in cages. I used to read, incredulous, about the crimes of the past. Now that we have our own concentration camps and ghettos, I am finished with history.

Sontag wrote, "Someone who is permanently surprised that depravity exists...when confronted with evidence of what humans are capable of inflicting in the way of gruesome, hands-on cruelties upon other humans, has not reached moral or psychological adulthood." One fall, not long ago, I grew up. The pumpkins, piled in cardboard boxes pitied me as I walked past. I no longer hold my tongue like the good girl I was taught to be, hair brushed and braided.

The waves beat the whale-watching boat and return me to the months I was pregnant and told not to end it. By my husband. By my mother. A woman has voted against all women and the Supreme Court is lost. I am safe on the cold beach picking shells. Every child on the sand knows this dilemma. The shells look perfect, cradled in the wet sand, before you bend and hold them to find each dull and dry in your hands. I stash a few in a tin with a watercolor of the lighthouse on the lid. I memorize the one I found so I know which is mine.

As Antigone—

When I understood
that you couldn't be
saved, all I had left
was the ability
to be good. To be right—
envied by everyone
who didn't have my courage
or conviction. I wasn't brave.

All I could do was curl up
next to your mute body
and burrow my face under
your lifeless arm. I needed
some way to quiet
your terrible voice.

As Antigone—

I know you always want
to hear the one about the moon,
not because it's celestial

but for the way it lets you say
goodbye. No shocking departure,
no tricks. Predictable, you

memorized it without trouble.
In bed alone, that big room
still looms—each familiar object

lined up to be named. Maybe
that's the comfort—to name
the way gods do. To look

upon the ordinary and form
new sounds in the mouth.
I named you eight years

before you were born, after
reading a book about a river
who was a girl who was a river.

I knew you would be dark
and dangerous like my mother,
my grandmother. I did what none

of them could do—I took you
to my breast, despite your family's
curse. When I hold your bulky body,

shame disappears. Even the moon
listens as I sing to you—
so strange is my simple voice.

No one will ever love you
as much. If your mother were stronger,
she could take care of your daughter
forever. All that adoration and no mind
of her own to form an opinion different
from hers. O, she would be better than a garden—
all the hostas and daylilies lined up to greet her
as she walks out the back door.

Memento Mori: Northern White Rhinos

They are grey, big as boulders,
gentle as the grass they spend
the whole day grazing. The only two
left of their kind, mother and daughter—
they live under armed guard
in a Kenyan sanctuary,
after spending their life caged
in a Czech zoo.

Unaware of their doom,
they pass their last days eating
and napping. Each time they lower
their heavy bodies down to rest—
they sleep, tusks touching. Love,
what do any of us have but this?

Memento Mori: Muleteer of Pompeii

You have inhabited me
since I first saw you. At twenty-two,
I wanted to pull back the bars
between us—crawl to you
past the amphora, over the garden
of fugitives. Thousands of years
too late, I longed to hold you
as you hid your face in your hands.

I didn't know my life
would be spent comforting
a creature like you,
hands over her ears—
always secreting herself
from my voice.

Memento Mori: Buried Children of Tuam

One cannot marry an Irishman without uncovering skeletons.
Only once did my first husband's grandmother show me
the biscuit tin of photographs as we sat above the Limerick
family store. Even then, she didn't tell me her youngest sons
never spoke. That one died of pneumonia at four and the other
lived in a playpen until he was twelve and then carted off
to Dublin and left with nuns who pushed him through parks
in a wheelbarrow until he died at twenty-six.

Even after you didn't speak, your father's family said nothing.
When you were finally diagnosed, an aunt whispered the truth.
Showed me clippings from her brother's asylum. In those photos,
your great-uncle smiles into the distance the way you do as I sing
nursery rhymes to you in your yellow room. You are as beautiful
as all the abandoned children of Tuam, awaiting their first communion.

November

Venice is flooding. Not just aqua alta but waves in the center of San Marco. Gondolas sit like beached whales in the thin alleys. The cathedral has flooded six times in twelve centuries—three times in two years. Italy is the first country to require climate change to be taught in schools. The pigeons are gone, the "eat & flee tourists" walk, waist-deep, in three feet of water. Merchants can't afford to live here, travel from Mestre to pack their masks and marionettes. One dies pumping water from his shop.

I spent two weeks in Venice at the end of the last century. While the rest of the world worried about Y2K, the Italians drank wine and sold crackled wooden cherubs to tourists. I searched for Carpaccio's Saint George slaying the dragon in a scuola with a thick velvet curtain that matched the color of dragon blood. When I left the city, I was pregnant. It only took four weeks for the nausea to begin. The nurses ran IV fluids four times in three months and I thought I was drowning. I lost thirty-three pounds. The doctors promised me the baby would be healthy. They were wrong. At nineteen, she still babbles more than she speaks, takes six medications that can't stop her seizures. The doctors no longer apologize. They leave me to my own research. She is 160 times more likely to drown, her life expectancy is thirty-six years.

Virginia Woolf left a letter to her husband before she filled her pockets with stones and walked into the river. "What I want to say is I owe all the happiness of my life to you...if anybody could have saved me it would have been you. Everything has gone from me but the certainty of your goodness."

The last time I walked that city, young boys handed out pamphlets shouting, "Vivaldi concert tonight." Their jackets were the blue of Giotto's sky. The first thing I bought for my daughter's nursery was a personified crescent moon facing the sun. It hung above her door for ten years—gold and silver, fighting for her attention. It took time to realize why she hated its eyes and mouth, its long nose. It didn't resemble the drawing from her favorite book. The one she has said *good night* to six thousand times. It didn't match her one vision of the moon.

November

We unplugged the old television. It started humming on Tuesday night and after three days, turned into an incessant rumble. The news still seeps in. I go from one doctor's appointment to another—mine, my daughter's, mine. The meditation instructor says, with practice, we can learn to tolerate our commute. Her voice first annoys then soothes me. I listen to the same three songs on loop as I wait for my biopsy results. Across the country, my doctor friend is dying of breast cancer. It no longer matters how much science she knows. Eighteen years ago, I visited her daughter in the hospital, hours after she crashed into the world, screaming.

In *The Second Sex*, Simone de Beauvoir wrote, "A woman is shut up in a kitchen or a bedroom, and one is surprised her horizon is limited; her wings are cut, and then she is blamed for not knowing how to fly."

It's Election Day again and I cast my vote early in the dilapidated school up the block. Just last month, I stood in the middle of my favorite green field. Time collapsed; I was seventeen, I was forty-six. Light lifted gold leaves from the herringbone bricks beyond the gate. I sat in a stiff chair and listened again to the voice that lit four years of darkness before I read my own work to young women who watched me. At home, my favorite store announces a going-out-of-business sale. The rent in Chelsea is too high. Never again will I see the ceramic doll heads stacked one top of another in a tall, glass vase.

Creon Creates His Own Truth

It took me years to see the chaos
he wanted to create—he brought

blight to the roses and cut them
back to claim the cure. All summer,

he set small fires with words
but kept his hands clean.

He turned us against each other
as if we were all invasive species

in his groomed garden. As we sat
under the golden rain tree, I worried

the sliver of moon would incur
his wrath for its imperfection.

Fear is an addictive drug. When
he fits his tight fist around my throat

now, I hear his lies as lies. My crime
is thinking for myself. Hannah Arendt

believed forgiveness is the key
to freedom. I cannot agree.

You are not wrong
about the leader.
He lives for performance
and propaganda.
Memes, mockery, morality
will not thwart him.

Memento Mori: Winter

For some, it's a skull, sitting sideways
on a side table, smooth as ice. For me—
snow, stacked still and stately on the sidewalk,
deceptive as promises. It stalks me
all winter, yet I refuse to fly away
to warmer climates. It whispers what happened
that February—a spun car, the unbelted driver
who took our youth with him into his stiff coffin.

I know how it feels to be a tree stump, unmovable
as the oak's thick bark, suffocated by snow.
Whenever I see white, I wonder how I resisted
all the drugs, incidental and prescribed,
that taunted me for decades. After each surgery,
I wean myself off the small pills the color of angels' wings.

Memento Mori: Ice Storm

Black as the estuary at night,
eleven crows fly past my bay window
just ahead of the storm. Years ago,
I would have thought them portentous.
Now, I understand what's random
and what's real. As I read the news,
ice falls from the sill above and it shatters,
like your diagnosis, on the sidewalk.

Too late, I see a sign in front of the church
that cautions, in red marker, about falling ice.
No warning proves sufficient for the danger
of walking through this world. Two traffic lights
outside my window alternate signals all night—
red and green. *Stop, go. Stay, run away.*

February

This has always been the month of death I tell the dog as my oldest friend dies on her daughter's birthday. I try not to think of the June evening we ate across from the Acropolis our last night in Athens. Twenty-two years ago, the only tragedies we knew were those from books we studied in school. We bought the same make-up and sunglasses—so young, we didn't know we didn't need them. My daughter wakes at four a.m. from a fever and echoes what I whisper to console her. On my birthday, she's too sick to go to school and sleeps all day. I walk her to the bakery for a croissant and sing in the dark to keep her calm.

Beckett wrote, "Memories are killing. So you must not think of certain things, of those that are dear to you, or rather you must think of them, for if you don't there is the danger of finding them, in your mind, little by little."

I let myself think of Georgia as I break from work. I sift through the photo box from grad school—the first wedding in Kastoria, the pensione in the mountains where the walls were so thin, we could hear each other breathe. For years, I was envious of her healthy daughters. After we were both in remission, she drove me to Sonoma for a mud bath. We stood together in the shower as big as a studio, our scars white and jagged as the path we drove in the Peloponnesus to get to the sea. She said we were cured but I thought we were living on borrowed time. Nobody is ever right about anything.

As Antigone–

I'm all done being nice.
It hasn't gotten me anywhere.

Since I was young, I gave
everything away—milk

money, homework, adoration.
Everyone wanted to make me

into a small version of herself—
teaching me weaving, writing,

wiles. All I wanted was love—
picked a bouquet of dandelions

and handed it to my mother.
When she turned her mouth

into a little *o* and called the tight
yellow suns *weeds*, my body

became a weight I wanted
to let go. I thought of all

the lessons I memorized
to keep me still, the colors

I couldn't wear because
they clashed with my red hair,

all the rules of modesty
so men would not look at me

with hunger. The only thing
I owned was a jar I was given,

like Pandora, as a girl. Before I
unlatched the lid, I had already lost

everything—faith, health,
my child. I refused to watch

what flew out. But something
hard as lapis, real as want,

wrenched my wrist right back
so hope remained, writhing

alone at the bottom of the jar
like dirty water after dead

tulips are discarded—
yellow stamens dropping

pollen to the floor. Silent,
it watched me for years.

Months at a time, I forgot
it was there. But when it's

trapped like that, it grows
so large, nothing can quell it.

No one thanks me for what
I have done. But I don't need

praise anymore. I turned
weeds into flowers.

As Antigone—

I enter the tomb and learn
what nothing is. The rain-
drenched body, its broken

kneecaps. My sour stench
escaped from the bay window,
grew wings, and left me. I paint

angels, not for protection
but for the face I never had.
Their eyes turn up as if

there were a sky. Running
through the woods, I foresaw
this death—propped up

wicked and hollow, like plastic
storefront mannequins.
The women I adore attach

their shoulders to their chins—
demure, demure. Once flesh
is locked up, it belongs

to the pure cold of earth.
I'm glad my uncle did this.
It proves he never loved me—

all his words were lies. Vigils
are obsolete. Don't tell me
where to place my candles.

Memento Mori: Stradivarius

In a few decades, they will go to sleep. Even
the greatest instruments must die; their wounded
wood will no longer make the same sounds they've made
for three centuries. The mayor of Cremona shuts the town,
blocks the cobblestone streets for five weeks so musicians
can record thousands of scales and arpeggios in quiet.
Each car remains parked and silenced; all the buzzing
lightbulbs in the concert hall stand unscrewed.

I love the citizens of my grandparents' home,
believing humans will still be alive to hear music.
I want them to play these recordings
as the world ends, each unique violin reaching out
to the great concert hall of the universe—
all the unoccupied velvet chairs.

Memento Mori: Forced Retirement

My grandfather has made and destroyed statues
for two decades. He believes gradually giving away
everything in his house will postpone death. God seems
to agree to this pact but he hides things from God.
There are hundreds of lamps still to go—filling
the walk-in closet, jutting out from coats—once statues,
once vases, once his wife's candelabra. Bronzed
and shellacked, he has fathered a little army of illumination.

Angelo, I am just like you—remaking the world we are given.
I watched you paint your dying cactus green. After you drill
your father's tie pin into the thick varnish of the boy's inner elbow,
you hand me the bronze baby Jesus, curly hair frozen
in windblown stupor. Jesus sits blissfully legs in mid-dangle,
cradling a little skull with dimmed rhinestone eyes.

Memento Mori: Mourning Mother

In this dark room of ruins, I want to take your stony face
in my hands. The boy you made is gone. Silent as these statues
and as still, you're at home among the shards and symbols,
casting spells on those left living who abandoned him. You cannot
accept that we betray the dead. All the large and little lies. Excuses
the living make not to crawl into the grave beside them. Mothers
are fastened to suffering but scholars tell us to move on, pretending
grief is the narrow path in Delphi that leads to the Pythia.

Your face is Jocasta's the moment before she screamed. I wore
your expression in the neurologist's office, my damaged baby
sprawled at my feet—all curls and flesh, sturdy as my Sicilian
ancestors. Everyone promises your pain will recede
but they're wrong; you will not heal. You'll only endure life
from now on—your boy's words perpetual Kaddish on your open lips.

March

The three of us have seen only each other for eleven days. Our fevers are low-grade but I am the only one who coughs through the night. Under each window, the city is empty as the moon. Sirens startle the bruised sky and my father doesn't believe we're in danger. From Sappho's work, we have fragments—"what cannot be said will be wept." Imagine if we could behold her, whole. The doctor upstairs cannot calm her children. They trample the wooden floors but it sounds more like hammering nails into coffins. News, news, charts, news. My mother sends photos of her pear trees—subject line: nothing can stop spring. I've started bargaining. Oh, the things I have given up in the crook of night. The books beg to be opened. Sappho wrote, "Someone, I tell you, in another time will remember us."

My students flatten to faces on a screen. Musicians play to an empty theatre. I scroll past memes of Dickinson as saint of social distancing and unfriend everyone who claims we don't need to wear masks. An occasional headline praises the plague-time productivity of Shakespeare. The rest report job loss, exploitation of essential workers, death counts. Three drinks in, my brother texts with grim predictions while I try to read twelve pages of *War & Peace* for an online book club, sprung up overnight. Two kinds of cancer grow in my father, his surgery suspended while they ready the hospital for hundreds of patients who can't breathe. For fifteen years, the plague doctor's beaked mask from Venice hung on my wall but I left it, hanging from its black string, when I moved out. I try to sleep with two inhalers and a stack of books perched beside me. Like a spell, I write a list of everyone I want to save and repeat their names while the dog sleeps beside me. I start and end with you. It's already morning in Italy; quarantined neighbors sing from open windows.

As Antigone—

I am waiting for biopsy results again—
in the mirrored room where time stalls.
Women are always at the mercy of men.
Even after I get the results, it will feel like my fault.

In the mirrored room where time stalls,
I stare at the same insipid face.
Even after I get the results, it will feel like my fault.
I walk the treadmill, regretting what I can't erase.

I stare at the same insipid face.
The longer I carry my body, the harder it is to tend.
I walk the treadmill, regretting what I can't erase.
Until I die, this worry will never end.

The longer I carry my body, the harder it is to tend.
Women are always at the mercy of men—
until I die, this worry will never end.
I am waiting for biopsy results again.

As Antigone—

I realize why I love the dead. They are
the only ones who cannot betray me.
I talk to them without judgment. They have
said every cruel thing they will utter, stolen
everything they will take. Finished fighting
their flawed battles, they are as tired as I am,
crumpled in the corner of my bed—hiding
my eyes under a silver sheet. They are quiet;

their closed mouths stitched shut like the dolls
I wanted to smash against my bureau
after my mother lined them up around my room.
I recite lines to them to prove I'm not alone.
Sometimes, I hear them echo my words back to me
while the moon watches with its rough, cold face.

The Climate Clock says there are six years
one hundred fifty-three days, nine hours,
fifty-eight minutes, eight seconds to rescue
the earth from irrevocable disaster.

Memento Mori: Mentor with Late-Stage
Lewy Body Dementia

for Richard Howard

The greatest mind I ever met now sits stiff
in a rented wheelchair. His hands seem to sew
invisible thread as his husband and I talk on a bench
in his courtyard. Like his beloved Penelope, weaving
endlessly on her loom only to pull her work apart each night,
he sits in turn patient and perturbed by something
we cannot see. He looks up at me only twice,
both times disappointed I am not someone else.

Across the courtyard, hydrangeas bloom,
oblivious and blue. His bent fingers grasp the hem
of my dress he once would have loved. I want him
to talk about his paused translation. I want to sit
next to him on his small sofa as he reaches for a book—
for him to mark these lines with his sharp black pen.

Memento Mori: Medieval Scribe

She toiled in silence on manuscripts. Maybe
in a scriptorium with a view of green,
a splash of white for sheep or cloud,
depending on the season. She presided
over her paints whose colors, to her,
were more like words. Archaeologists
find lapis lazuli between her teeth and prove
women, too, illuminated manuscripts.

Imagine her kneeling at a wooden table—
in candlelight, at dawn, drawing the tip of the fine
brush through her lips to make it finer still. Listen
to her sigh, as her open mouth cradles ultramarine
that will hide in the cracks of her teeth for centuries,
blue as a pharaoh's death mask. Deep as angels' robes.

Memento Mori: Aleppo

Let me learn a little
of your grace from the way
you threw your tired body
over the incubators
as the air strikes came—
the *best pediatrician*
in the *most dangerous city*
in the world.

Let me learn a little of your grace
in this city where we are alive
but only some are safe.
I honor you as I bend
my tired body and hold
my dying child's face.

May

America's new disease and old disease keep killing. The names of the dead fill the newspapers. Only some of us are safe. This country was stolen—built on blood and lies. History is not the past. On the news, the president denies everything we know to be true. Orwell wrote, "The party told you to reject the evidence of your eyes and ears. It was their final, most essential command." In a slanted room, the stone-hearted judge plots with the single-minded precision of a serial killer. White candles burn down to the wick and the succulents need to be replanted. Since you can't sleep, you read about exploding stars in supernovas that scattered the calcium of all human bones and teeth. And how Stephen Hawkings proved there is no God. My friend's son asks, whenever he hears sirens, if cops are coming to kill him. My daughter's brain is stuck at twenty months, trapped in her body of nineteen years. She doesn't yet know about hatred but, someday, her silence will destroy her. We cannot be saved but I wish some god would save them. The cherry trees are about to flower. The buds are small bloody fists.

As Antigone–

I contemplate my choices
at 4:32 a.m. and go back to the first—
the one that married me

to suffering and sleep deprivation.
Go back to the hospital bed
with tubes wrapped around me

as if I were a gift. Return
to the moment a psychiatrist
stood above my bed like a sentry

because I wanted to end the life
inside me to stop the hyperemesis—
incessant vomiting. Let's go back

to the moment my mother
convinced me to put myself last
as mothers have been doing

to daughters for millennia. Recall
her eyes as they watched me sign
my release papers. Let's return

to the silent drive back to the house
she bought for me and my new
husband and unpacked her suitcase

to nurse me for thirteen weeks
and make sure I didn't slink back
to the hospital in an ambulance

and end it the way I wanted to.
Let's return to that room where
I could have stood up to her

and said she was not the one
being ravaged by illness, not
the one who lost thirty-three pounds.

That she would not have to raise
the child if something went wrong.
Go back to the disinfectant,

the cornflower blue gowns.
The nurses pricking my hands
with needles. Go back

to the moment before I would
always be controlled by my mother,
by my daughter. Go back

to the moment I realize my mother
will never apologize for what
she has done. Go back. Back, back.

Now that I love my daughter,
there is no way out. Not even if I tie
my own dress around my neck.

When you said you know
you are not a narcissist
because you are a masochist,
your first psychiatrist reminded you
about Jesus and how you
made your way through Italy
collecting small souvenirs
of wooden angels and gilded
reproductions of Madonna
and Child to hang on your walls
to punish you.

As Antigone–

I see my hubris. Tulips
turn to late winter sky

like shelter dogs wanting
to go home. *I'm waiting,*

I'm waiting, they whisper
while I speak tender words

to the dead. Those who cannot
speak are most worthy of words.

In love with the impossible
and certain I am right,

I go inside and close the door.
I know how to be alone.

To be a character in a tragedy,
you must be blind to your flaw.

I always look at the world
from windows. The park,

a green canopy, hovers
against the blue. In this wind,

the unhinged door on the roof
across the street opens, bangs shut.

You are nothing more than a lone tulip
trying to stand erect in the wild wind.

Memento Mori: Partnering a Runner

You will never know what he thinks about while he runs,
as music muffles the city's roar of evening, yawn of morning.
As he smells burnt leaves in autumn, spring petrichor, the river
in summer. You cannot imagine how trees are always more
themselves as he passes their leaves over and over again
during an eight-minute mile. See the sky as he does—watch it
change from the smeared palette of the old watercolorist
beside the Kyoto temple to Michelangelo's dark frescos.

Think of his stories—the starting gun in high school, his two
nicknames. Don't pretend to understand what pulls him out
in all weather at the clock's every hour while the ruined earth turns
and his knees grow older. Realize what you make seeks the same
elusive god. Never ask what he's looking for on the streets and bridges
of his city. Know this chase that keeps him will keep him here.

Memento Mori: Pistachios

I never know I'm an animal more
than when I shell pistachios in the kitchen,
after washing dishes, waiting for you to come
home. I know how I must look, cracking
the tight shells, popping the small green nut
into my open mouth again and again.
I never knew your trick to pry a stubborn
shell—slit not wide enough to open.

You showed me how to place half
a discarded shell in the small opening,
like a tool. It frightens me—
my new resourcefulness. My hunger.
The way I wait for you as if
I will never have enough.

October

Even though we have done nothing wrong, as we cross state lines, we feel guilty. Being inside an apartment for six months straight makes me dangerous. The light interrogates us as we drive out of the city, north to the Cape. The ducks and herons greet us with their calls, monitoring the inlet all night as we lie awake, glad to be tucked into strange thin sheets. The dog sits by my feet and watches waterfowl walk back and forth on the dock, next to a tree more similar to a cypress than any other that can grow in New England. I put my phone in the drawer so the news cannot claim me. Still, I hear the tyrant is in the hospital and as soon as he's released, he makes his men drive him through the streets though he's still contagious. The woman who wants to repeal Roe v. Wade will be confirmed before the election. It all comes through as static, as indistinct as my friend in Trinidad reading his poems from his aqua room.

Here, I wake early, sit on the small deck with a mug of strong coffee, read the new novel by the writer with whom I rode the train in January. I live in her old building now. I don't care if she used part of my sad story to help make a case for euthanasia. That was my old life and I leave it here in the damp marshlands where the ducks skim the water in jagged rows. I watch light lace the trees. "The meaning of life is that it ends," Kafka wrote. At home, you bring me coffee in the mug smothered by Warhol's outlandish poppies—purple, red, purple.

November

We have aged nine years over the last four. Our dog and our daughter pace the living room, as if they know what hangs in the balance. I slice the apple and cut myself—watch the blood soak into the wooden cutting board as if it were not my own. The days are getting shorter. It is almost a hundred years since Celan was born and fifty since he drowned himself in the Seine, unused *Waiting for Godot* tickets in his wallet at home. Bill Irwin performs Beckett in a bowler hat and baggy pants—part clown, part clairvoyant. Celan said, "Only one thing remained reachable, close and secure amid all losses: language. In spite of everything, it remained secure against loss." Words kept him alive years after his mother was murdered. It doesn't diminish his words that he chose to stop speaking.

We go to sleep and wake up four times. Still the election has not been called. We find out the news the way our ancestors did in times of plague. Bells ring out in the streets and while we emerge from the cloying rooms, stale with old air, early autumn meets us like longed-for draft. We walk five miles. The dog drags behind us. We talk to strangers; the city is still our home. Since Celan, after all he witnessed, could write "a star still has its light. Nothing, nothing is lost," I must believe him. We enter the building through the side door and see no one. I wash and peel the ripe pears.

Memento Mori: Shelter Dog

In the year without, I learn from the quiet
dog who watches me as I work and read,
follows me from room to room in my small apartment,
runs and whimpers in her sleep. We leave the building
only to walk in the park, the trees marking months
like hungry mouths. Outside, her nose interrogates
the dirt, smelling the city. Memorizing morning.
When the tulips arrive, she breathes beside their slanted stems.

In June, we walk among the tall allium—two bumps
betray botched healing of her broken tail. I tell her
I have not accepted my daughter's devastating damage
or the weekly seizures that render her speechless.
Watching her is the closest I will ever come to prayer.
Every night, the dog puts her head on my stomach and sighs.

Memento Mori: Empty Frames at the
Isabella Stewart Gardner Museum

On green and yellow walls the gilded rectangles hang,
framing absence. It's the first thing you see
as you enter each room—the space where
the Vermeer or the Rembrandt should be. Worn
damask wallpaper calls attention to the loss
of what was once there. Gardner's will insists
nothing can change after her death, so the frames hang,
empty, as if they are waiting for the art to come home.

You touch my hand, thinking of my diagnosis
and impending surgery. We both know one of these scares
will not be a false alarm. I watch you stand before the space
where the concert should hang. You still see
the harpsichord and lute. You can even hear the woman
breathe, as she opens her mouth about to sing.

Memento Mori: Lovers of Valdaro

This is what I want. Nothing else will do but to tie our bodies
together in one final embrace so our bones lace together,
leaving the archeologists to wonder whose they were.
Not our nightly burrowing from behind, my back sliding
into your chest, feeling you against me, tempting you to stay
awake. This last time, we would lie face to face so I could breathe
my last breaths looking into your autumnal eyes. I want to believe
there is field full of poppies where we will walk again but I have
grown tired of stories that defer living to some imagined afterlife.

My friend says we are lucky we didn't meet
while we were young—there will be no time to weary
of each other's words or mouths. Under glass in a museum,
the lovers of Valdaro remain, their skulls seem to smile.
Like a finely carved instrument, their bones, silent
as violin strings, wait for the touch that releases song.

June 24, 2022

That alabaster hospital room—for twenty-two years, I have tried to crawl my way out. Its antiseptic smells and white walls still taunt me as I read today's headlines and think of all the women and girls now stripped by the state of their right to choose. I begged them—first my mother, then my husband. Then together. I cried, hair matted and dirty from vomiting for twenty-three days. Seven weeks pregnant, I pleaded with them not to force me to have the baby. As if my body already knew how sick she was and how the architecture of my life would be destroyed. Instead of helping me, my husband ordered a psych consult. He was a doctor so he convinced the attending that I was hysterical and didn't know my own mind. Anyone with a mind knows this has always been about control.

Nothing is enough. I offer to help women travel here and bring them to clinics, write postcards to swing states—my body a sanctuary and a shrine. Because I love my daughter more than myself, there are some decisions I can never come back from. Dickinson wrote, "To attempt to speak of what has been, would be impossible. Abyss has no Biographer—" My daughter crumbles like a rag doll when she seizes—her heavy body limp in my arms. I watch us from above, our forced and permanent *Pietà*. Can you see the truth? The child isn't the one who is dead.

As Antigone–

I still want to believe
        I can find some way
to fix you. That if I go

back to the beginning—
        retrace the disaster
with the savant detective's

obsession, I could uncover
        a cure—the smartest
expert, some successful drug.

Better yet, I want
        the pediatrician
to give you a different diagnosis.

I want to go back
        to the walk home
past restaurants and playgrounds,

autumnal light catching
        all the auburn
in your hair. I want to go back

to the moment
        your father left us
outside the cafe, consider

handing you to him—
        all forty-seven pounds
of you in your gingham pants

and hot pink cardigan—
        Dalmatians decorating
the little pockets—and walk away

without looking back.
        But I would never have left
and I won't now. One way

or another, you will
        be the end of me—
inadvertent brute force,

vector of virus, constant
        caretaking, your heavy
body forcing my remission's

abrupt end. I know
       what's waiting—
as certain as cloth hung to hold

my scarred neck.
       I will not walk away.
The moment the nurse

pressed your splotched
       body into my arms,
your needs fixed my fate.

Constantly confused,
       your jagged voice
requests Christmas songs

all spring. You shove
       words of grace
into my dry throat

and I sing. I don't need
       a bottle of pills,
white as sleep, to silence me.

Every ersatz saint knows
        endless sacrifice
is suicide. For twenty years,

I have been disappearing.
        Touch me;
I am not even here.

Acknowledgments:

The author would like to thank the editors of the following publications in which these poems have appeared, some in earlier versions:

American Poetry Review, The Academy of American Poets *Poem-a-day* Series, *Barrow Street*, *Beloit Poetry Journal*, *Bennington Review*, *Blackbird*, *Broadsided Press*, *Cordella Review*, *The Cortland Review*, *Drunk Monkeys*, *Gettysburg Review*, *JAMA*, *Juniper*, *Lily Poetry Review*, *Los Angeles Review*, *Love's Executive Order*, MER VOX folio, *New Verse News*, *The Night Heron Barks*, *Nixes Mate Review*, *On the Seawall*, *Ovenbird*, *Pigeon Pages*, *Plume*, Poetry in Motion, RI/Poetry Society of America, *Poetry Northwest*, *Poets Reading the News*, *Prometheus Dreaming*, *Ran off with the Star Bassoon*, *Re: (A Journal of Ideas)*, RHINO, *Salamander*, *The Scores*, *Sixth Finch*, *Small Orange Journal*, StatoRec, *Stone Canoe*, *upstreet*, *Valparaiso Poetry Review*, and *What Rough Beast/Indolent Books*.

Anthologies:

American Journal of Poetry: God & Monsters: "As Antigone—[I am tired of everyone telling me what to do...]"
Nixes Mate Anthology: "October [I try to keep the image of the sunset over the lighthouse at the edge of the Cape]"
Plume 8: "Memento Mori: Bird Head"
Plume 10: "Memento Mori: Mentor with Late-Stage Lewy Body Dementia"

Small Orange Journal Anthology: "Creon Creates His Own Truth"
Tree Lines: "Memento Mori: Apple Orchard"

Notes:

The book takes its title from a line in the chorus of Anne Carson's *Antigonick*, her translation of Sophokles's *Antigone*. "Blessed be they whose lives do not taste of evil / but if some god shakes your house / ruin arrives / ruin does not leave." Gratitude to Anne for all she has meant to this collection.

"Memento Mori: Wind Phone" was written after listening to the podcast, "One Last Thing Before I Go" from September 23, 2016 on NPR's "This American Life." This episode was about a disconnected phone in a booth in rural Japan where people speak to dead loved ones lost in the 2004 tsunami. It is for Richard McCormick, in memory of his mother, Ann McCormick.

"Memento Mori: Death Mask," was written at the Emily Dickinson Museum's "A Mighty Room" Virtual Studio Session in the Library, on Zoom on February 5, 2021.

"Memento Mori: Annunciation, without Angel" owes a debt to Colm Tóibín's novella, *The Testament of Mary* and the painting *The Virgin Annunciate*, a painting by the Italian Renaissance artist Antonello da Messina of Sicily.

"Memento Mori: Northern White Rhinos" was written after reading "The Last Two Northern White Rhinos on Earth: What will we lose when Najin and Fatu die?" by Sam Anderson in *The New York Times*, January 6, 2021.

"Memento Mori: Buried Children of Tuam" was provoked by Dan Barry's article, "The Lost Children of Tuam" in *the New York Times* on October 28, 2017. It details the suspicious deaths of children and their subsequent secret burial in the septic tank of a mother and baby home for children born "out of wedlock" in Tuam, County Galway, Ireland.

"February" is for Georgia Hatzivassiliou, Ph.D. (November 18, 1970-February 18, 2020).

"Memento Mori: Stradivarius" was written after reading "To Save the Sound of a Stradivarius, a Whole City Must Keep Quiet" by Max Paradiso in *The New York Times* on January 17, 2019.

"Memento Mori: Forced Retirement" is for Angelo Caiati. (March 17, 1912-June 15, 2005).

"Memento Mori: Mourning Mother" is for Ariella Ritvo-Slifka.

"Memento Mori: Mentor with Late-Stage Lewy Body Dementia" is for Richard Howard.

"Memento Mori: Medieval Scribe" was inspired by the article "Why a Medieval Woman Had Lapis Lazuli Hidden in Her Teeth" by Sarah Zhang in *The Atlantic* on January 9, 2019.

"Memento Mori: Aleppo" was written in memory of Dr. Muhammad Waseem Maaz, the Syrian pediatrician killed in an airstrike on al-Quds hospital on April 29, 2016.

"Memento Mori: Lovers of Valdaro" are a pair of human skeletons (a man and a woman) approximately 6,000 years old. They were discovered by archaeologists lead by Elena Maria Menotti at a Neolithic tomb near Mantua, Italy in 2007. They were buried face to face with their arms around each other reminding onlookers of a "lovers' embrace." They are permanently displayed inside a glass case in a museum in the Ducal Palace of Mantua.

Deep gratitude to—

My family—the love of my life, Richard McCormick; our sweet
daughter, Anna Livia; and our gentle rescue pitbull, Dottie. As
Merwin wrote, "I needed my mistakes / in their own order / to get
me here."

My parents—Anna & James Franklin for exposing me to books
from the earliest time, giving me the endless gift of my college and
graduate school education, and nurturing my dream to become a
writer. Thank you to my grandparents, Clara & Angelo Caiati who
helped to raise me and taught me what is truly important in life; my
brother, sister-in-law, and niece—Jim, Virginie, and
Emilie Franklin—for their camaraderie; my late mother-in-law,
Ann McCormick; my father-in-law, Richard McCormick; and my
aunt-in-law, Jackie Fantasia. Most of all, I appreciate each of you for
your love and loyalty to Anna Livia.

My peerless mentor Arnold Weinstein—endless admiration
and appreciation.

My late teachers especially Richard Howard who published my
first five poems. And to Michael S. Harper, C.D. Wright, David
Krause, Mark Spilka, Lucille Clifton, Lucie Brock-Broido, and Shane
Steck—as Franz Wright wrote, "I know dead people, and you are
not dead."

The astonishing poets who leant their words in support of this collection—Edward Hirsch, Deborah Paredez, and Diane Seuss.

My fellow writers, editors, and program directors who offered invaluable inspiration, feedback and/or support of this work: Lauren Acampora, Jenny Barber, Marion S. Brown, Nickole Brown, Chris Campanioni, Rafael Campo, Tina Cane, Susana H. Case, Christina Chiu, Dana Curtis, Kwame Dawes, Darren Demaree, Brian Komei Dempster, Alex Dimitrov, Gregory Donovan, Sean Thomas Dougherty, Rita Dove, Mark Drew, Michael Dumanis, Sally Bliumis-Dunn, Peggy Ellsberg, Patrick James Errington, Blas Falconer, Joan Falk, Karen Finley, Nick Flynn, Carolyn Forché, Rebecca Foust, Sandra M. Gilbert, Louise Glück, Jessica Greenbaum, Susan Gubar, Rachel Hadas, Carlie Hoffman, JP Howard, Marie Howe, Jessica Jacobs, Kirun Kapur, Rogan Kelly, Aaron Caycedo-Kimura, Ellen Kombiyil, Keetje Kuipers, Daniel Lawless, Matthew Lippman, Cynthia Manick, Lynn McGee, Erika Meitner, Kamilah Aisha Moon, Maddie Mori, Felice Neals, Miller Oberman, Suzanne Parker, Zeeshan Pathan, Oliver de la Paz, Annie Pluto, Iain Haley Pollock, Connie Post, Ruben Quesada, Spencer Reece, Frances Richey, Elizabeth Scanlon, Laurie Sheck, Neil Silberblatt, Sean Singer, Lori Soderlind, Andrew Solomon, Brooke Steinhauser, Margo Taft Stever, Arthur Sze, Mervyn Taylor, Leah Umansky, Afaa Michael Weaver, Justin Wymer, and Anton Yakovlev.

My beloved friends—Trish Abate & Luke Seigel; David Alexander; Anna Alperovich; Babis, Marina & Lydia Andreadis & Georgia

Hatzivassiliou; Ann, John, Avery & Ariana Brown; Paula Colangelo; Geoff Collins & Sandy Enuha; the Chun-Kwon-Pincus family; Rebecca Doverspike, Rosanne English; Lisa Ferri & Jim Edwards; Amanda Gersh; Beth Hahn; Anne Krause; Alison Lonshein; Kris Lowe & Brian Dunderdale; Fred Marchant & Stefi Rubin; Clayton Marsh; Massimo Maglione; Debbie Mitzner & Wayne L. Miller; Anna Krugovoy Silver, Betsy Tsai, Jeff Colt & Cooper Tsai-Colt; Max Ritvo & Ari Ritvo-Slifka; Ann Weiss; and Michelle Whittaker. My wonderful current and former students at the Hudson Valley Writers Center—Gayle Augenbaum, Vincent Bell, Carla Carlson, Roxanne Cardona, Susan Coronel, Ellen Devlin, Elizabeth Ehrlich, H.E. Fisher, Lisa Fleck, Sherine Gilmour, Alice Green, Caroline Holme, Tony Howarth, Barb Jennes, Luisa Caycedo-Kimura, Aubrey Moncrieffe, Beth Morris, Jack Powers, Michael Quattrone, Alice Campbell-Romano, Vera Salter, M.A. Scott, Lee Sennish, Rachael Phillips, Harriet Shenkman, Kristen Skedgell, Maria Surricchio, Sheila Rabinowitch, Kathryn Quinones, Kathryn Weld, Kathleen Williamson, and Ellen Wright.

All the teachers, board members, and students at the Hudson Valley Writers Center; the poets and volunteers at Slapering Hol Press; and my amazing colleagues at Manhattanville's MFA Program. Special thanks to the incredible team at HVWC—Sophia Bannister, Mary Carroll Linder, and Christina Papadopoulos.

The doctors and physical therapists who diagnosed me, supervised my recovery, and made me new: Dana Aaron, Louis Harrison, Mark

Persky, Peter Sherman, Sabrina Strickland, David Shapiro, and
Sylvester Wojtkowski.

Café Royal Cultural Foundation for supporting the final editing of
this manuscript.

NYFA & City Artist Corps for the poetry grant.
Martha Rhodes, Ryan Murphy, Sally Ball, Hannah Matheson,
Bridget Bell, and the entire team at Four Way Books for their
unwavering support and literary citizenship.

Jennifer Franklin is the author of two previous full-length poetry collections, most recently *No Small Gift* (Four Way Books, 2018). Her work has been published widely in print and online including, *American Poetry Review, Barrow Street, Beloit Poetry Journal, Bennington Review, Boston Review, Gettysburg Review, Guernica, JAMA, The Nation, New England Review, the Paris Review,* "poem-a-day" series for the Academy of American Poets on poets.org, *Prairie Schooner,* and *RHINO.* She received a City Corps Artist Grant in poetry from NYFA and a Café Royal Cultural Foundation Grant for Literature in 2021. For the past ten years, she has taught manuscript revision at the Hudson Valley Writers Center, where she runs the reading series and serves as Program Director. She also teaches in Manhattanville's MFA program. She lives with her husband and daughter in New York City. Her website is jenniferfranklinpoet.com.

Publication of this book was made possible by grants and donations. We are also grateful to those individuals who participated in our Build a Book Program. They are:

Anonymous (13), Robert Abrams, Michael Ansara, Kathy Aponick, Jean Ball, Sally Ball, Clayre Benzadón, Adrian Blevins, Laurel Blossom, adam bohannon, Betsy Bonner, Patricia Bottomley, Lee Briccetti, Joel Brouwer, Susan Buttenwieser, Anthony Cappo, Paul and Brandy Carlson, Mark Conway, Elinor Cramer, Dan and Karen Clarke, Kwame Dawes, Michael Anna de Armas, John Del Peschio, Brian Komei Dempster, Rosalynde Vas Dias, Patrick Donnelly, Lynn Emanuel, Blas Falconer, Jennifer Franklin, John Gallaher, Reginald Gibbons, Rebecca Kaiser Gibson, Dorothy Tapper Goldman, Julia Guez, Naomi Guttman and Jonathan Mead, Forrest Hamer, Luke Hankins, Yona Harvey, KT Herr, Karen Hildebrand, Carlie Hoffman, Glenna Horton, Thomas and Autumn Howard, Catherine Hoyser, Elizabeth Jackson, Linda Susan Jackson, Jessica Jacobs and Nickole Brown, Lee Jenkins, Elizabeth Kanell, Nancy Kassell, Maeve Kinkead, Victoria Korth, Brett Lauer and Gretchen Scott, Howard Levy, Owen Lewis and Susan Ennis, Margaree Little, Sara London and Dean Albarelli, Tariq Luthun, Myra Malkin, Louise Mathias, Victoria McCoy, Lupe Mendez, Michael and Nancy Murphy, Kimberly Nunes, Susan Okie and Walter Weiss, Cathy McArthur Palermo, Veronica Patterson, Jill Pearlman, Marcia and Chris Pelletiere, Sam Perkins, Susan Peters and Morgan Driscoll, Maya Pindyck, Megan Pinto, Kevin Prufer, Martha Rhodes, Paula Rhodes, Louise Riemer, Peter and Jill Schireson, Rob Schlegel, Yoana Setzer, Soraya Shalforoosh, Mary Slechta, Diane Souvaine, Barbara Spark, Catherine Stearns, Jacob Strautmann, Yerra Sugarman, Arthur Sze and Carol Moldaw, Marjorie and Lew Tesser, Dorothy Thomas, Rushi Vyas, Martha Webster and Robert Fuentes, Rachel Weintraub and Allston James, Abigail Wender, D. Wolff, and Monica Youn.